FEDERALISM UNMASKED:

OR THE RIGHTS OF THE STATES, THE CONGRESS, THE EXECUTIVE, AND THE PEOPLE, VINDICATED AGAINST THE ENCROACHMENTS OF THE JUDICIARY, PROMPTED BY THE MODERN APOSTATE DEMOCRACY. BEING A COMPILATION FROM THE WRITINGS AND SPEECHES OF THE LEADERS OF THE OLD JEFFERSONIAN REPUBLICAN PARTY.

BY DANIEL R. GOODLOE

The following are the authorities quoted:

THOMAS JEFFERSON.

These extracts from Jefferson's writings can be verified by reference to the index to his complete works, published under the patronage of Congress. The reader is referred to the names of the persons to whom the letters are addressed.

In a letter to Mr. Adams, dated September 11, 1804, he says:

You seemed to think that it devolved on the judges to decide on the validity of the sedition law. But nothing in the Constitution has given them a right to decide for the Executive, more than the Executive to decide for them. Both magistrates are equally independent in the sphere of action assigned to them. The judges, believing the law constitutional, had a right to pass a sentence of fine and imprisonment; because the power was placed in their hands by the Constitution. But the Executive, believing the law to be unconstitutional, were bound to remit the execution of it; because that power had been confided to them by the Constitution.

Extract of a letter to Judge Roane, dated Poplar Forest, September 6, 1819.

In denying the right they usurp of exclusively explaining the Constitution, I go further than you do, if I understand rightly your quotation from the Federalist, of an opinion that "the Judiciary is the last resort in relation *to the other departments* of the Government, but not in relation to the rights of the parties to the compact under which the Judiciary is derived." If this opinion be sound, then, indeed, is our Constitution a complete *felo de se.* For, intending to establish three departments, co-ordinate and independent, that they might check and balance one another, it has given, according to this opinion, to one of them alone the right to prescribe rules for the government of the others; and to that one, too, which is unelected by and independent of the nation.

* * * The Constitution, on this hypothesis, is a mere thing of wax, in the hands of the Judiciary, which they may twist and shape into any form they please. It should be remembered, as an axiom of eternal truth in politics, that whatever power in any Government is independent, is absolute also; in theory only at first, while the spirit of the people is up, but in practice as fast as that relaxes. Independence can be trusted nowhere but with the people in mass. They are inherently independent of all but moral law. My construction of the Constitution is very different from that you quote. It is, that each department is truly independent of the others, and has an equal right to decide for itself what is the meaning of the Constitution in the cases submitted to its action, and especially

where it is to act ultimately and without appeal. I will explain myself by examples, which, having occurred while I was in office, are better known to me, and the principles which governed them.

Extract from a letter to Mr. Jarvis, dated Monticello, September 28, 1820.

* * * You seem, in pages 84 and 148, to consider the judges as the ultimate arbiters of all constitutional questions—a very dangerous doctrine indeed, and one which would place us under the despotism of an oligarchy. Our judges are as honest as other men, and not more so. They have, with others, the same passions for party, for power, and the privilege of their corps. Their maxim is, "*boni judicis est ampliare jurisdictionem*," and their power the more dangerous as they are in office for life, and not responsible, as the other functionaries are, to the elective control. The Constitution has erected no such single tribunal, knowing that, to whatever hands confided, with the corruptions of time and party, its members would become despots. It has more wisely made all the departments co-equal and co-sovereign within themselves. If the Legislature fails to pass laws for a census, for paying the judges and other officers of the Government, for establishing a militia, for naturalization, as prescribed by the Constitution, or if they fail to meet in Congress, the judges cannot issue their mandamus to them; if the President fails to supply the place of a judge, to appoint other civil or military officers, to issue requisite commissions, the judges cannot force him. They can issue their mandamus or distringas to no executive or legislative officer, to enforce the fulfilment of their official duties, any more than the President or Legislature may issue orders to the judges or their officers.

Extract from a letter to Thomas Ritchie, dated Monticello, December 25, 1820.

* * * The Judiciary of the United States is the subtle corps of sappers and miners constantly working under ground to undermine the foundations of our confederated fabric. They are construing our Constitution from a co-ordination of a general and special government to a general and supreme one alone.

Extract from a letter to Archibald Thweat, dated Monticello, January 19, 1821.

The Legislative and Executive branches may sometimes err, but elections and dependence will bring them to rights. The Judiciary branch is the instrument which, working like gravity, without intermission, is to press us at last into one consolidated mass. Against this I know no one who equally with Judge Roane himself possesses the power and the courage to make resistance; and to him I look, and have long looked, as our strongest bulwark. If Congress fails to shield the States from dangers so palpaple and so imminent, the States must shield themselves, and meet the invader foot to foot. This is already half done by Colonel Taylor's book, because a conviction that we are right accomplishes half the difficulty of correcting wrong. This book is the most effectual retraction of our Government to its original principles which has ever yet been sent by Heaven to our aid. Every State in the Union should give a copy to every member they elect, as a standing instruction, and ours should set the example. Accept, with Mrs. Thweat, the assurance of my affectionate and respectful attachment.

Extract from a letter to Mr. C. Hammond, dated Monticello, August 18, 1821.

It has long, however, been my opinion, and I have never shrunk from its expression, (although I do not choose to put it into a newspaper, nor, like a Priam in armor, offer myself its champion,) that the germ of dissolution of our Federal Government is in the constitution of the Federal Judiciary—an irresponsible body, (for impeachment is scarcely a scarecrow,) working like gravity by night and by day, gaining a little to-day and a little to-morrow, and advancing its noiseless step, like a thief, over the field of jurisdiction, until all shall be usurped from the States, and the Government of all be consolidated into one. To this I am opposed; because, when all government, domestic and foreign, in little as in great things, shall be drawn to Washington as the centre of all power, it will render powerless the checks provided of one Government on another, and will become as venal and oppressive as the Government from which we separated. It will be as in Europe, where every man must be either pike or gudgeon, hammer or anvil. Our functionaries and theirs are wares from the same workshop, made of the same materials, and by the same hand. If the States look with apathy on this silent descent of their Government into the gulf which is to swallow all, we have only to weep over the human character, formed uncontrollable but by a rod of iron, and the blasphemers of man, as incapable of self-government, become his true historians.

Extract from a letter to William T. Barry, dated Monticello, July 2, 1822.

Sir: Your favor of the 15th of June is received, and I am very thankful for the kindness of its expressions respecting myself. But it ascribes to me merits which I do not claim. I was only of a band devoted to the cause of Independence, all of whom exerted equally their best endeavors for its success, and have a common right to the merits of its acquisition. So, also, is the civil revolution of 1801. Very many and very meritorious were the worthy patriots who assisted in bringing back our Government to its Republican tack. To preserve it in that, will require unremitting vigilance. *Whether the surrender of our opponents, their reception into our camp, their assumption of our name, and apparent accession to our objects, may strengthen or weaken the genuine principles of Republicanism, may be a good or an evil, is yet to be seen.* I consider the party division of Whig and Tory the most wholesome which can exist in any Government, and well worthy of being nourished, to keep out those of a more dangerous character. We already see the power, installed for life, responsible to no authority, (for impeachment is not even a scarecrow,) advancing with a noiseless and steady pace to the great object of consolidation.

The foundations are already deeply laid, by their decisions, for the annihilation of constitutional State rights, and the removal of every check, every counterpoise, to the engulphing power of which themselves are to make a sovereign part. If ever this vast country is brought under a single Government, it will be one of the most extensive corruption, indifferent and incapable of a wholesome care over so wide a spread of surface. This will not be borne, and you will have to choose between reformation and revolution. If I know the spirit of this country, the one or the other is inevitable. Before the canker is become inveterate, before its venom has reached so much of the body politic as to get beyond control, remedy should be applied. Let the future appointments of judges be for four or six years, and renewable by the President and Senate. This will bring their conduct, at regular periods, under revision and probation, and may keep them in equipoise between the general and special Governments. We have erred in this point, by copying England, where certainly it is a good thing to have the judges independent of the King. But we have omitted to copy their caution, also, which makes a judge removable on the address of both legislative houses. That there should be public functionaries independent of the nation, whatever may be their demerit, is a solecism, in a Republic, of the first order of absurdity and inconsistency.

Extract from a letter to Judge Johnson, dated Monticello, March 4, 1823.

I cannot lay down my pen without recurring to one of the subjects of my former letter, for, in truth, there is no danger I apprehend so much as the consolidation of our Government by the noiseless, and therefore unalarming, instrumentality of the Supreme Court. This is the form in which Federalism now arrays itself; and consolidation is the present principle of distinction between Republicans and pseudo-Republicans, but real Federalists. I must comfort myself with the hope that the judges will see the importance and the duty of giving their country the only evidence they can give of fidelity to its Constitution, and integrity in the administration of its laws; that is to say, by every one's giving his opinion *seriatim* and publicly on the cases he decides. Let him prove by his reasoning that he has read the papers; that he has considered the case; that, in the application of the law to it, he uses his own judgment independently, and unbiassed by party views and personal favor or disfavor. Throw himself in every case on God and his country; both will excuse him for error, and value him for his honesty. The very idea of cooking up opinions in conclave, begets suspicions that something passes which fears the public ear; and this, spreading, by degrees must produce at some time abridgment of tenure, facility of removal, or some other modification which may promise a remedy. For, in truth, there is at this time more hostility to the Federal Judiciary than to any other organ of the Government.

I should greatly prefer, as you do, four judges to any greater number. Great lawyers are not over-abundant, and the multiplication of judges only enable the weak to out-vote the wise; and three concurrent opinions, out of four, gives a strong presumption of right.

Extract from a letter to Judge Johnson, dated Monticello, June 12, 1823.

The practice of Judge Marshall, of travelling out of his case to prescribe what the law would be in a moot case not before the court, is very irregular and very censurable. I recollect another instance, and the more particularly, perhaps, because it in some measure bore on myself. Among the midnight appointments of Mr. Adams were commissions to some Federal justices of the peace for Alexandria. These were signed and sealed by him, but not delivered. I found them on the table of the Department of State, on my entrance into office, and I forbade their delivery. Marbury, named in one of them, applied to the Supreme Court for a mandamus to the Secretary of State, (Mr. Madison,) to deliver the commission intended for him. The court determined at once, that being an original process, they had no cognizance of it; and, therefore, the question before them was ended. But the Chief Justice went on to lay down what the law would be, had they jurisdiction of the case, to wit: that they should command the delivery. The object was clearly to instruct any other court, having the jurisdiction, what they should do, if Marbury should apply to them. Besides the impropriety of this gratuitous interference, could anything exceed the perversion of law? For if there is any principle of law never yet contradicted, it is, that delivery is one of the essentials to the validity of a deed. Although signed and sealed, yet as long as it remained in the hands of the party himself, it is *in fieri* only—it is not a deed, and can be made so only by its delivery. In the hands of a third person, it may be made an escrow. But whatever is in the Executive offices is certainly deemed to be in the hands of the President; and in this case was actually in my hands, because, when I countermanded them, there was as yet no Secretary of State. Yet this case of Marbury and Madison is continually cited by bench and bar, as if it were settled law, without any animadversion on its being merely an *obiter* dissertation of the Chief Justice. * * *

But the Chief Justice says, "there must be an ultimate arbiter somewhere." True, there must; but does that prove it is either party? The ultimate arbiter is the people of the Union, assembled by their deputies in Convention, at the call of Congress, or of two-thirds of the States. Let them decide to which they mean to give an authority claimed by two of their organs. And it has been the peculiar wisdom and felicity of our Constitution to have provided this peaceable appeal, where that of other nations is at once to force.

Extract from a letter to Edward Livingston, Esq., dated Monticello, March 25, 1825.

I have attended to so much of your work as has been heretofore laid before the public, and have looked with some attention also into what you have now sent me. It will certainly arrange your name with the sages of antiquity. Time

5'5 3

and changes in the condition and constitution of society may require occasional and corresponding modifications. One single object, if your provision attains it, will entitle you to the endless gratitude of society—that of restraining judges from usurping legislation. And with no body of men is this restraint more wanting than with the judges of what is commonly called our General Government, but what I call our foreign department. They are practicing on the Constitution by inferences, analogies, and sophisms, as they would on an ordinary law. They do not seem aware that it is not even a *Constitution* formed by a single authority, and subject to a single superintendence and control, but that it is a compact of many independent powers, every single one of which claims an equal right to understand it and to require its observance. However strong the cord of compact may be, there is a point of tension at which it will break. A few such doctrinal decisions as barefaced as that of the Cohens, happening to bear immediately on two or three of the large States, may induce them to join in arresting the march of Government, and in arousing the co-States to pay some attention to what is passing, to bring back the compact to its original principles, or to modify it legitimately by the express consent of the parties themselves, and not by the usurpation of their created agents. They imagine they can lead us into a consolidated Government, while their road leads directly to its dissolution. This member of the Government was at first considered as the most harmless and helpless of all its organs. But it has proved that the power of declaring what the law is, *ad libitum*, by sapping and mining, slily and without alarm, the foundations of the Constitution, can do what open force would not dare to attempt.

Extract from a letter to Mr. W. H. Torrance, dated Monticello, June 11, 1815.

The second question, whether the judges are invested with exclusive authority to decide on the constitutionality of a law, has been heretofore a subject of consideration with me in the exercise of official duties. Certainly there is not a word in the Constitution which has given that power to them more than to the Executive or Legislative branches. Questions of property, of character, and of crime, being ascribed to the judges through a definite course of legal proceeding, laws involving such questions belong, of course, to them; and as they decide on them ultimately, and without appeal, they, of course, decide for *themselves.* The constitutional validity of the law or laws again prescribing executive action, and to be administered by that branch ultimately, and without appeal, the Executive must decide for *themselves*, also, whether, under the Constitution, they are valid or not. So also, as to laws governing the proceedings of the Legislature, that body must judge *for itself* the constitutionality of the law, and equally without appeal or control from its co-ordinate branches. And, in general, the branch which is to act ultimately, and without appeal, on any law, is the rightful expositor of the validity of the law, uncontrolled by the opinions of the other co-ordinate authorities. It may be said that contradictory decisions may arise in such case, and produce inconvenience. This is possible, and is a necessary failing in all human proceeding, yet the prudence of the public functionaries and authority of public opinion will generally produce accommodation.

In vol. 9, page 464, I find a series of resolutions, which the editor thinks were the original of the famous Kentucky resolutions relative to the alien and sedition laws:

1. *Resolved*, That the several States comprising the United States of America are not united on the principle of unlimited submission to their General Government, but that, by a compact under the style and title of a Constitution for the United States, and of amendments thereto, they constituted a General Government for special purposes—delegated to that Government certain definite powers, reserving, each State to itself, the residuary mass of right to their own self-government; and that whensoever the General Government assumes undelegated powers, its acts are unauthoritative, void, and of no force; that to this compact each State acceded as a State, and is an integral party, its co-States forming, as to itself, the other party; that the Government created by this compact was not made the exclusive or final judge of the extent of the powers delegated to itself, since that would have made its discretion, and not the Constitution, the measure of its powers; but that, as in all other cases of compact among powers having no common judge, each party has an equal right to judge for itself, as well of infractions, as of the measure and mode of redress.

8. *Resolved*, * * * That in cases of an abuse of the delegated powers, the members of the General Government being chosen by the people, a change by the people would be the constitutional remedy; but where powers are assumed which have not been delegated, a nullification of the act is the rightful remedy; that every State has a natural right, in cases not within the compact, (*casus non fœderis*,) to nullify, of their own authority, all assumptions of power by others within their limits; that without this right they would be under the dominion, absolute and unlimited, of whosoever might exercise this right of judgment for them; that, nevertheless, this Commonwealth, from motives of regard and respect for its co-States, has wished to communicate with them on the subject; that with them alone it is proper to communicate, they alone being parties to the compact, and solely authorized to judge, in the last resort, of the powers exercised under it, Congress being not a party, but merely the creature of the compact, and subject, as to its assumptions of power, to the final judgment of those by whom, and for whose use, itself and its powers were all created and modified.—*Page* 469.

RESOLUTIONS OF 1798, DRAWN BY MADISON.

In the Virginia House of Delegates, Friday, December 21st, 1798:

Resolution 3. That this Assembly doth explicitly and peremptorily declare, that it views the powers of the Federal Government, as resulting from the compact to which the States are parties, as limited by the plain sense and intention of the instrument constituting that compact, as no farther valid than they are authorized by the grants enumerated in that compact; and that in case of a deliberate, palpable, and dangerous exercise of other powers not granted by the said compact, the States, who are parties thereto, have the right, and are in duty bound, to interpose, for arresting the progress of the evil, and for maintaining within their respective limits the authorities, rights, and liberties, appertaining to them.

Resolution 5. That the General Assembly doth particularly protest against the palpable and alarming infractions of the Constitution in the two late cases of the "alien and sedition acts," passed at the last session of Congress; the first of which exercises a power nowhere delegated to the Federal Government, and which, by uniting legislative and judicial powers to those of executive, subverts the general principles of free government, as well as the particular organization and positive provisions of the Federal Constitution; and the other of which acts exercises, in like manner, a power not delegated by the Constitution, but on the contrary expressly and positively forbidden by one of the amendments thereto—a power which, more than any other, ought to produce universal alarm, because it is levelled against the right of freely examining public characters and measures, and of free communication among the people thereon, which has ever been justly deemed the only effectual guardian of every other right.

Resolution 7. That the good people of this Commonwealth, having ever felt, and continuing to feel, the most sincere affection for their brethren of the other States, the truest anxiety for establishing and perpetuating the Union of all, and the most scrupulous fidelity to that Constitution which is the pledge of mutual friendship and the instrument of mutual happiness, the General Assembly doth solemnly appeal to the like dispositions in the other States, in confidence that they will concur with this Commonwealth in declaring, as it does hereby declare, that the acts aforesaid are unconstitutional; and that the necessary and proper measures will be taken by each for co-operating with this State, in maintaining, unimpaired, the authorities, rights, and liberties, reserved to the States respectively, or to the people.

1798, December 24. Agreed to by the Senate.

JOHN TAYLOR OF CAROLINE.

John Taylor of Caroline, Va., was the Cato of the old Republican party, and his writings possessed almost oracular authority among the followers of Jefferson:

Extracts from "New Views of the Constitution," by John Taylor of Caroline, Virginia.

The perseverance of the gentlemen in favor of a National Government proves that the subject was thoroughly considered; and the solemn preference of the federal form demonstrates that no construction by which the preference will be frustrated can be just. Its basis was State sovereignty, compatible with a federal limited Government, but incompatible with a supreme National Government. Hence State sovereignty was denied by the gentlemen who proposed a National Government. This sovereignty is the foundation of all the powers reserved to the States. Unless they are sustained by it, they are baseless. State legislative, executive, and judical powers, must all or none flow from this source. All are necessary to sustain the State republican Governments. Subject either to a master, and the others become subject to the same master. If the State judicial power, as flowing from State sovereignty, is not independent, State legislative and executive power cannot be independent, because all rest upon the same foundation; and because, if a supreme federal Judiciary can control State courts, it can also control State Legislatures and Executives. Thus a federal form of government would be rejected, though it was established, and a National Government would be established, though it was rejected. * * *

The second section of the article we are considering begins with the following words: "The judicial power shall *extend.*" The word extend, far from meaning supremacy, implies the reverse. The distinction is expressed in the first article. The legislation of Congress is not *extended* to the ten miles square, but made supreme over that District, in order to abolish a State concurrency of power within it. The powers of Congress are extended to specified objects; but, as these extensions did not imply supremacy, the powers bestowed are concurrent, except when attended by positive prohibitions upon the States.—*See page* 130.

No legislative, executive, or judicial power, is given to the States, for enabling them to exercise their reserved rights, because they were derived from their anterior sovereignty. From this source, and the special delegations, arose many cases of a concurrency in State and Federal legislation, such as that of taxation; and this concurrency would have extended to all the delegated powers, except for the prohibitions of the tenth section of the first article. Those in relation to war, troops, and imports and exports, would have been useless, except that the States, in virtue of their sovereignty, would have retained an absolute power as to these objects, had no such prohibitions been inserted in the Constitution. They might have declared war, raised armies, and imposed duties, though Congress might have done it also, upon the same ground that both the State and Federal Governments may tax. Now, if an extension of some sovereign powers of the States to Congress did not, without a special prohibition, take from the States their right to exercise the same powers, the Constitution itself furnishes us with a construction of the judicial article. As the extension of legislative Federal power to taxation did not destroy the sovereign power of the States to tax, nor invest Congress with a supreme power to annul State laws for that purpose, so the extension of the Federal judicial power to cases in law and equity, arising under the Federal Constitution and laws, did not deprive the States of the inherent attribute of sovereignty to dispense justice to their people in these cases, nor expose their decisions in cases of law and equity to be annulled by the Federal Judiciary. A concurrency of jurisdiction arose from the extension of judicial Federal power, upon the same principles which produced a concurrency of legislation between the Federal and State Governments. Original sovereignties were not in either case surrendered to a delegated participation. It is owing to a concurrency of jurisdiction in the Federal and State Governments, that the judges of both are required to take an oath to support the Constitution; and this concurrency is distinctly admitted by the Federal judges in revising State judgments, and affirming them, if right; whereas, if the State courts had no jurisdiction in cases of law and equity arising under the Federal Constitution and laws, all their judgments would have been *coram non judice*, and void. Their jurisdiction is thus admitted, and the only question is, whether Congress can empower the Federal court to annul it.—*Pages* 131, 132.

Controversies may arise under the Constitution between political departments, in relation to their powers; between the legislative and treaty-making departments; between the Senate and the House of Representatives; between the President and the Senate, or between the State and Federal departments; but they would not be cases in law and equity, nor is any power to decide them given to the Federal Judiciary. One species of controversy relates to the form of government; the other flows from its operation. The power by which a Government is formed or altered is not the power by which the lawsuits of individuals are tried; and therefore a power to try suits in law and equity was never supposed to comprise the former powers.

Among the cases to which the Federal jurisdiction is extended, not one is to be found recognising a power to decide controversies between any of these political departments. It is inconceivable that a jurisdiction, transcending beyond comparison the jurisdiction cautiously specified, should have been tacitly given without any specification.—*See pages* 134, 135.

The third article of the Constitution is both organic and legal—organic, in establishing a Federal Judiciary; legal, in creating several new individual legal rights; but its legal character, to be discerned in this and other articles, is addressed to all individuals, and of course to all tribunals. The mechanism of a supreme and inferior courts does no more create a supreme national judicial power, than the mechanism of Congress can create a supreme national legislative power. None of these wheels or pullies were intended to destroy the State Governments, or their republican forms, or the reservation by which only life is infused into those forms. Hence the mechanism of the Federal courts into supreme and inferior was only intended as an auxiliary towards enforcing the legal character of the Constitution, and not as an instrument for altering its organic or its contracting characters. The Constitution, as a law, would produce cases in law and equity. To such cases only, and not to the principles of the compact, nor to the mechanism of our system, the judicial power of the United States is extended. The State courts may also try cases in law and equity, but this gives them no power to alter the mechanism or principles of Constitutions, or to determine the controversies of political departments. Authorities might be cited, in great numbers, to prove that such powers have never been considered as annexed to a jurisdiction in cases of law and equity, but only a Federal and State construction is adduced. Congress have given to the courts of Columbia a power to try *all cases in law and equity*. Do these words convey a power to regulate the political departments or principles by which the District is governed? The States gave to the Federal courts the same power. Do the same words convey a power to regulate the political departments or principles by which the States are governed, and not those by which Columbia is governed? The State of Ohio gave a jurisdiction to one *supreme* court and *inferior* courts, in *cases of law and equity*. Did this create a jurisdiction able to regulate the powers of political departments created by its Constitution?—*Pages* 138, 139.

The legal feature of the Constitution, in relation to judges, is expressed in the sixth article: "The Constitution is the *supreme law* of the land, and the judges in *every State* are to be bound thereby." Can the judgments of the Federal court be a supreme law over this supreme law? Is there no difference between the supremacy of a Federal court over inferior Federal courts, and the supremacy of the Constitution over all courts? The supremacy of the Constitution is a guaranty of the independent powers, within their respective spheres, allowed by the Federalist to the State and Federal Governments. A supremacy in the court might abridge or alter these spheres. The State judges are bound by the Constitution and by an oath to obey the supremacy of the Constitution, and not even required to obey the supremacy of the Federal court. Why are all the departments of the State and Federal Governments equally bound to obey the supremacy of the Constitution? Because the State and Federal Governments were considered as checking or balancing departments. Had either been considered as subordinate to a supremacy in the other, it would have been tyrannical to require it by an oath to support the supremacy of the Constitution, and also to break that oath by yielding to the usurped supremacy of the other. The oath requires loyalty to State and Federal powers; judgments might require disloyalty to both. The answer to this dilemma is, that as the Federal, in its mechanism, is a perfect Government, because it somewhat resembles the British, the States are bound to consider whatever it does as constitutional; and that therefore the oath, though taken in fact to support the Constitution, virtually binds the swearer to support both the laws of the Federal Government and the judgments of its Supreme Court. But since the State Governments, by their organization and by the guaranty, are considered as perfect Governments also in relation to their reserved powers, I do not see why the Federal Government is not, by the same virtual interpretation of the oath, bound to support State laws and judgments. Is it not as obvious, by endowing the Federal Government or either of its departments with this virtual supremacy over the State Governments, deduced, not from the principles of the compact, but from the form of its organization, that a consolidated National Government and a destruction of the State Governments would ensue, as by endowing the State Governments, upon the same grounds, with an unexpressed supremacy over the Federal Government, a dissolution of the Union would be the consequence? The fact is, that both are perfect Governments, in relation to their respective powers, subject in one case to three-fourths of the States, and in the other to the people of each State; and that neither this species of perfection, nor the mechanism of either, invests one with any species of supremacy over the other.—*See pages* 140, 141.

On Remodelling the Judiciary.

Near the close of the Administration of the elder Adams, viz: on the 13th February, 1801, the judiciary system was remodelled, by which a large number of circuit judgeships were created, and the Supreme Court made simply a court of appeal from the inferior jurisdictions. But a revolution had taken place in the politics of the country. Mr. Jefferson had been elected President, and his Republican friends had a majority in both branches of the succeeding Congress. Early in the session, Mr. Breckinridge, of Kentucky, introduced a resolution into the Senate, proposing the repeal of the judiciary act above referred to, which, after protracted debate in both branches of Congress, was carried.

MR. JACKSON, OF GEORGIA.

On the 12th January, Mr. Jackson, of Georgia, said:

We have been asked if we are afraid of having an army of judges? For myself, I am more afraid of an army of judges, under the patronage of the President, than of an army of soldiers. The former can do us more harm. They may deprive us of our liberties, if attached to the Executive, from their decisions; and from the tenure of office contended for, we cannot remove them; while the soldier, however he may act, is enlisted, or if not enlisted, only subsisted for two years; whilst the judge is enlisted for life, for his salary cannot be taken from him.—*See 12th division, 8th sec., 1st art., Constitution.*

Sir, it is said these evils will not happen. But what security have we for the truth of the declaration? Have we not seen sedition laws? Have we not heard judges crying out, through the land, sedition! and asking those whose duty it was to inquire, is there no sedition here? It is true, the sedition law had expired with the last Administration, and he trusted it would not exist, or at least be acted on, under the virtuous Jefferson. But hereafter, if it should exist, your judges, under the cry of sedition and political heresy, may place half your citizens in irons.—*See Annals of Congress*, 1801–'2, *page* 47.

STEVENS THOMPSON MASON, OF VIRGINIA.

During the same discussion, Mr. Mason, of Virginia, said:

The objects of courts of law, as I understand them, are to settle questions of right between suitors, to enforce obedience to the laws, and to protect the citizens against the oppressive use of power in the Executive offices. Not to protect them against the Legislature, for that I think I have shown to be impossible, with the powers which the Legislature may safely use and exercise, and because the people have retained in their own hands the power of controlling and directing the Legislature, by their immediate and mediate elections of President, Senate, and House of Representatives.—*See ib., page* 73.

MR. COCKE, OF TENNESSEE.

Mr. Cocke, of Tennessee, on the same subject, said:

We have been told that the nation is to look up to these immaculate judges to protect their liberties; to protect the people against themselves. This was novel, and what result did it lead to? He shuddered to think of it. Were there none of these judges ready to plunge their swords in the American heart? He did not think it proper to be alarmed by the terrors held out.—*Ib., page* 75.

THOMAS T. DAVIS, OF KENTUCKY.

In the House of Representatives, Mr. Davis, of Kentucky, said:

I found my opinion of the expediency of repealing the judiciary law on another reason in addition to that of the courts being unnecessary; I mean the power they declare they have, in the language of Judge Patterson, to "declare a law null and void." Never can I subscribe to that opinion. Never can I believe the Judiciary paramount to both branches of the Legislature; if it is, I have yet to learn it; there is an end to legislation; a knave or a fool can make void your best and most wholesome laws. * * * I am willing to admit the Judiciary to be coordinate with the Legislature in this respect, to wit: that judges, thinking a law unconstitutional, are not bound to execute it; but not to declare it null and void. That power rests alone with the Legislature. But we are told this Judiciary is necessary to check this House and the Senate, and to protect the people against their worst enemies. This is saying to the people, you are incapable of governing yourselves; your representatives are incapable of doing it; in the

Judiciary alone you find a safe deposit for your liberties; and saying, also, that the Judiciary is the vitals of the nation, wherein all power, all safety dwells; that the Legislature is subordinate thereto, and a mere nominal thing, a shadow without substance, its acts perfectly within the control of the Judiciary. I tremble at such ideas. The sooner we put men out of power, who we find determined to act in this manner, the better; by doing so, we preserve the power of the Legislature, and save our nation from the ravages of an uncontrolled Judiciary.—*Ib., page* 558.

WILLIAM B. GILES, OF VIRGINIA.

On the same subject, in the House of Representatives, Mr. Giles, of Virginia, said:

The general disquietude which manifested itself in consequence of these enterprising measures, in the year 1800, induced the Federal party to apprehend that they had pushed their principles too far, and they began to entertain doubts of the result of the Presidential election, which was approaching. In this state of things, it was natural for them to look out for some department of the Government in which they could entrench themselves in the event of an unsuccessful issue in the election, and continue to support those favorite principles of irresponsibility which they could never consent to abandon.

The Judiciary department, of course, presented itself as best fitted for their object, not only because it was already filled with men who had manifested the most indecorous zeal in favor of their principles, but because they held their offices by indefinite tenures, and of course were further removed from any responsibility to the people than either of the other departments. * *

Although the gentleman from New York (Mr. T. Morris) yesterday observed that the President had commenced a system of persecution, so ignorant, he said, he was, of the existence of such a system, that he could not conceive to what the gentleman alluded. It is some time, Mr. Chairman, since a member of this House, and sundry printers throughout the United States, have been amerced and imprisoned to appease the vengeance of an unconstitutional sedition act, for merely publishing their own sentiments, which happened to be unpalatable to the then existing Administration! It is some time, sir, since we have seen judges, who ought to have been independent, converted into political partisans, and, like Executive missionaries, pronouncing political harangues throughout the United States! It is some time, sir, since we have seen the zealous judge stoop from the bench to look out for more victims for judicial vengeance! It is some time since we have seen the same judicial impetuosity drive from the bar the most respectable counsel, who humanely proposed to interpose between a friendless and unprotected man and the judicial vengeance to which he was doomed! It is some time, sir, since we have seen the same judicial zeal extending the provisions of the sedition act, by discovering that it had jurisdiction of the *lex non scripta*, or common law. * * *

The first clause declares there shall be a Congress, to whom the business of legislation is confided. This Congress is to consist of a House of Representatives, to be chosen by the people immediately, and responsible to them at the end of every two years; and a Senate to be chosen by the Legislatures of the different States, who are chosen by the people—one-third of the Senators to be chosen every two years, and responsible at the end of every six years. The Executive power is vested in a President, who is chosen by electors, who are chosen for the express purpose by the people, and responsible at the end of every four years. * * *

Thus, then, are formed two departments, their powers specified and defined, the times for extending their powers fixed, and, indeed, a complete organization for the execution of their respective powers, without the intervention of any law for that purpose. A third department, to wit: the Judiciary department, is still wanting. Is that formed by the Constitution? How is that to be formed? It is not formed by the Constitution. It is only declared that there shall be such a department; and it is directed to be formed by the other two departments, who owe a responsibility to the people. Here there arises an important difference of opinion between the different sides of this House. It is contended on one side that the Judiciary department is formed by the Constitution itself. It is contended on the other side that the Constitution does no more than to declare that there shall be a Judiciary department, and directs that it shall be formed by the other two departments, under certain modifications. Article third, section first, of the Constitution, has these words: "The judicial power of the United States shall be vested in one Supreme Court, and in such inferior courts as Congress shall from time to time ordain and establish." Here, then, the power to ordain and establish inferior courts is given to Congress in the most unqualified terms, and also to ordain and establish "one Supreme Court." The only limitation upon the power of Congress in this clause consists in the number of Supreme Courts to be established; the limitation is to the number of one, although that is an affirmative and not a negative expression. The number of judges, the assignation of duties, the fixing compensations, the fixing of times when, and places where, the courts shall exercise their functions, &c., are left to the entire discretion of Congress. The spirit as well as the words of the Constitution are completely satisfied, provided one Supreme Court be established. Hence, when all these essential points in the organization and formation of courts is intrusted to the unlimited discretion of Congress, it cannot be said that the courts are formed by the Constitution. * * *

The Legislature has no more control over an officer who holds an executive commission during the pleasure of the President, than over a judicial officer holding his office during good behaviour—the remedy given by the Constitution being the same in both cases, to wit: impeachment. Nor is there any reason why the office of the one should be less subject to the discretion of the Legislature than the office of the other; and it seems to be universally agreed, that although the Legislature cannot deprive an Executive officer of his office in any other way than by impeachment, during the continuance of such office, yet the office itself is always subject to be abolished. The same reasoning will hold with equal force respecting a judge and a judicial office. The reason why the Executive is proscribed from the removal of a judge, is to secure to the judge a complete independence of the President, who is not responsible for the discharge of judicial duties; but the removal is perfectly correct in the case of an Executive officer, because the President is highly responsible for the due discharge of Executive duties. The Legislature is not responsible for either, and, of course, stands in the same constitutional relation to both. * * *

And in this part of the sentence, the correct phraseology of the Constitution is worthy of observation. In speaking of the Executive attribute, to wit: the appointing and commissioning officers, the term *good behaviour* is used. In speaking of the legislative attribute, to wit: the creation of the offices, and fixing compensations, the term *during their continuance in office* is used. The reason for this variation of expression is obvious. It was known that the office might be discontinued, and the judge continue to behave well; the limitation was therefore applied to the office, and not to the good behaviour, because if the office should be discontinued, which is clearly implied in this expression, it was not the intention of the Constitution that the compensation should be received, no service in that event being to be rendered.

Can so much inattention and folly be attributed to the framers of the Constitution as would result from the supposition that if it was their intention that a law growing out of the specified powers, in contradistinction to all others, should be irrepealable when once passed, that so extraordinary a principle would be left to mere implication? Such a supposition would be the highest injustice to the superior intelligence and patriotism of those gentlemen, manifested in every other part of the instrument. No, sir; they would have made notes of admiration; they would have used every mark, adopted every caution, to have arrested and fixed the attention of the Legislature to so extraordinary a principle. They would have said, Legislators, be circumspect! Be cautious! Be calm! Be deliberate! Be wise! Be wise, not only for the present, but be wise for posterity! You are now about to tread upon holy ground. The law you are now about to pass is irrepealable! irrevocable! We are so enamored with the salutary and practical independence of the English judiciary system, that, in infusing its principle into our Constitution, we have stamped it with the proverbial folly of the Medes and Persians! If this principle had been introduced into the Constitution in express words, it would have formed an unfortunate contrast to all other parts of the instrument; yet gentlemen make no difficulty in introducing that principle by construction, which would have appeared so stupid and absurd if written in express words in the body of the instrument. * * *

But the most important consequence from this doctrine is, that it erects the judges into a body politic and corporate, in perpetual succession, with censorial and controlling powers over the other departments. And for what purpose? The gentleman from North Carolina (Mr. Henderson) has informed us, "to protect the people against their worst enemies—themselves!" This is the real exposition of the object, in very few but emphatical words. * * *

Very shortly after the establishment of courts, the judges decided that they had jurisdiction over the States in their sovereign capacity. Did this, in the judges, seem unambitious? The States thought it did not. * * *

The judges have determined that they are judges, in the last resort, upon the constitutionality of your laws. He proposed not to discuss this question, because he did not think it pertinent to the question before us. He only mentioned it to show their unlimited claims to power. The judges have determined that their jurisdiction extends to the *lex non scripta*, or rather to the *lex non descripta*, or common law. Does this, in the judges, seem unambitious? This law pervades the whole municipal regulations of the country. It is unlimited in its object, and indefinite in its character. Legalize this unassuming claim of jurisdiction by the judges, and they have before them every object of legislation. They have sent a mandatory process, or process leading to a mandamus, into the Executive Cabinet, to examine its concerns. Does this, in the judges, seem unambitious? Now, sir, examine and combine the extraordinary pretensions to power; legalize them, and you have precisely that body politic and corporate which gentlemen deem so important in the United States, "to protect the people from their worst enemies—themselves!" He should not revert so frequently to this expression, but that he did consider it as the candid and correct exposition of the object of gentlemen opposed to the repeal. It was the doctrine of irresponsibility against the doctrine of responsibility. The latter, he had endeavored to show, characterized the Constitution of the United States. It was the doctrine of despotism, in opposition to the representative system. It was an express avowal that the people were incompetent to govern themselves.—*Ib., pages* 581—596.

ROBERT WILLIAMS.

Robert Williams, of North Carolina, said:

That there must be some place where the true meaning of the Constitution must be determined, all would agree. Where, then, is it? In what department? The people have constituted two departments of authority — the Executive and Legislative, emanating directly from the people—and have directed them to form another, farther removed from the people. Are we, then, to be told there is more safety in confiding this important power to the last department, so far removed from the people, than in departments flowing directly from the people, responsible to, and returning at short intervals into, the mass of the people? * * *

If this doctrine is to extend to the length gentlemen contend, then is the sovereignty of the Government to be swallowed up in the vortex of the Judiciary. Whatever the other departments of the Government may do, they can undo. You may pass a law, but they can annul it. Will not the people be astonished to hear that their laws depend upon the will of the judges, who are themselves independent of all law?—*Ib., pages* 531, 532.

JOHN RANDOLPH.

John Randolph, of Roanoke, said:

But, sir, if you pass the law, the judges are to put their veto upon it by declaring it unconstitutional. Here is a new power, of a dangerous and uncontrollable nature, contended for. The decision of a constitutional question must rest somewhere. Shall it be confided to men immediately responsible to the people, or to those who are irresponsible? for the responsibility by impeachment is little less than a name. From whom is a corrupt decision most to be feared? To me it appears that the power which has the right of passing, without appeal, on the validity of your laws, is your sovereign. * * * But, sir, are we not as deeply interested in the true exposition of the Constitution as the judges can be? With all the deference to their talents, is not Congress as capaple of forming a correct opinion as they are? Are not its members acting under a responsibility to public opinion, which can and will check their aberrations from duty? Let a case, not an imaginary one, be stated: Congress violates the Constitution by fettering the press; the judicial corrective is applied to; far from protecting the liberty of the citizen, or the letter of the Constitution, you find them outdoing the Legislature in zeal; pressing the common law of England to their service where the sedition law did not apply. Suppose your reliance had been altogether on this broken staff, and not on the elective principle? Your press might have been enchained till doomsday, your citizens incarcerated for life, and where is your remedy? But if the construction of the Constitution is left with us, there are no longer limits to our power; and this would be true, if an appeal did not lie through the elections, from us to the nation, to whom alone, and not a few privileged individuals, it belongs to decide, in the last resort, on the Constitution. Gentlemen tell us that our doctrine will carry the people to the gallows, if they suffer themselves to be misled into the belief that the judges are not the expositors of the Constitution. Their practice has carried the people to infamous punishment, to fine and imprisonment; and had they affixed the penalty of death to their unconstitutional laws, judges would not have been wanting to conduct them to the gibbet. * * * No, sir, you may invade the press; the courts will support you, will outstrip you in zeal to further this great object; your citizens may be imprisoned and amerced, the courts will take care to see it executed; the helpless foreigner may, contrary to the express letter of your Constitution, be deprived of compulsory process for obtaining witnesses in his defence; the courts, in their extreme humility, cannot find authority for granting it; but touch one cent of their salaries, abolish one sinecure office which the judges hold, and they are immediately arrayed against the laws, as the champions of the Constitution. Lay your hands on the liberties of the people, they are torpid, utterly insensible; but affect their peculiar interest, and they are all nerve. They are said to be harmless, unaspiring men. Their humble pretensions extend only to a complete exemption from legislative control, to the exercise of an inquisitorial authority over the Cabinet of the Executive, and the veto of the Roman Tribunate upon all your laws, together with the establishing any body of laws which they may choose to declare a part of the Constitution. * * * In their inquisitorial capacity, the Supreme Court, relieved from the tedious labor of investigating judicial points by the law of the last session, may easily direct the Executive, by mandamus, in what mode it is their pleasure that he should execute his functions. They will also have more leisure to attend to the Legislature, and forestall, by inflammatory pamphlets, their decisions on all important questions; whilst, for the amusement of the public, we shall retain the right of debating, but not of voting.—*Ib., pages* 661, 662.

NATHANIEL MACON.

Nathaniel Macon, of North Carolina, said:

We have heard much about the judges, and the necessity of their independence. I will state one fact, to show that they have power as well as independence. Soon after the establishment of the Federal courts, they issued a writ—not being a professional man, I shall not undertake to give its name—to the Supreme Court of North Carolina, directing a case then depending in the State court to be brought into the Federal court. The State judges refused to obey the summons, and laid the whole proceedings before the Legislature, who approved their conduct, and, as well as I remember, unanimously; and this in that day was not called disorganizing.—*Ib., page* 711.

JOSEPH H. NICHOLSON.

Joseph H. Nicholson, of Maryland, said:

This Judiciary, however, the gentleman from Delaware has said, in that same spirit of Christion meekness which appears to have characterized him throughout, he never considered a sanctuary, because he knew that nothing was sacred in the eyes of infidels. * * * If the entire rejection of the odious principle, that the reins of Government are to be placed in the hands of a set of men who are independent of and beyond the control of the people, afford any evidence of infidelity, then do I avow myself as much an infidel as any man living. * * *

Have the people of this country ever consented to vest the judges with this extensive discretionary power? Have they ever sanctioned the principle that the judges should make law for them instead of their Representatives? Is it not legislation, to all intents and purposes, when your judges are authorized to introduce at pleasure the laws of a foreign country, to arm themselves with power? The American people never dreamed of such a principle in the Constitution, and never will submit to it. They never ought to submit to it. It is giving to the judges a power infinitely more transcendent than that vested in any other branch of the Government. The Legislature cannot recognise any principle of the common law having a monarchical tendency; yet this principle the judges may recognise if you leave it to their discretion to introduce any part of the common law which they may think proper. * * *

By what authority are the judges to be raised above the law and above the Constitution? Where is the charter which places the sovereignty of this country in their hands? Give them the powers and the independence now contended for, and they will require nothing more; for your Government becomes a despotism, and they become your rulers. They are to decide upon the lives, the liberties, and the property, of your citizens; they have an absolute veto upon your laws, by declaring them null and void at pleasure; they are to introduce at will the laws of a foreign country, differing essentially with us upon the great principles of government; and, after being clothed with this arbitrary power, they are beyond the control of the nation, as they are not to be affected by any laws which the people by their representatives can pass. If all this be true, if this doctrine be established in the extent which is now contended for, the Constitution is not worth the time we are now spending upon it. It is, as it has been called by its enemies, mere parchment; for these judges, thus rendered omnipotent, may overleap the Constitution, and trample on your laws; they may laugh the Legislature to scorn, and set the nation at defiance.

To me, it is a matter of indifference by what name you call them; I care not whether it be kings or judges. Arm them with power, and the danger is the same. For myself, I have no hesitation in declaring that I would rather be subject to the absolute sway of one tyrant, than to that of thirty; as I would prefer the mild despotism of China to the hated aristocracy of Venice, where the vilest wretch was encouraged as a secret informer, and the lion's mouth was ever gaping for accusation.—*Ib., pages* 805—824.

JOHN BACON.

John Bacon, of Massachusetts, said:

We have heard much of late about the peculiar and absolute independence of the Judiciary. Although this is a term unknown in the Constitution as applying particularly to the Judiciary department of the Government, yet it may and ought to be admitted to be, in a certain sense, and in some respects, true. The Judiciary are so far independent of the Legislative and Executive departments of the Government, that these, neither jointly or separately, have a right to prescribe, direct, or control, its decisions. It must judge for itself; otherwise the decisions made in that department would not be the decisions of that, but of some other department or body of men. The Constitution, and the laws made pursuant thereto, are the only rule by which the Judiciary, in their official capacity, are to regulate their conduct. The same is the case with other departments. The Judiciary have no more right to prescribe, direct, or control, the acts of the other departments of the Government, than the other departments of the Government have to prescribe or direct those of the Judiciary.—*Ib*, *page* 983.

THE SEDITION LAW—MATTHEW LYON'S CASE.

Matthew Lyon, of the State of Vermont, was convicted under the sedition act, in 1798, sentenced to several months' imprisonment, and the payment of a thousand dollars fine. He subsequently removed to Kentucky, and petitioned Congress more than once for indemnity, on the ground that the law under which he suffered was unconstitutional, as well as in consequence of irregularity in the proceedings of the court against him. On Tuesday, December 8, 1818, the memorial being under consideration in the United States Senate—

The Hon. John J. Crittenden, of Kentucky, said:

He considered the sedition act as having been unconstitutional, not only from a defect of power in Congress to pass such a law, but because its passage was expressly forbidden by the Constitution. The sense of the nation had unquestionably pronounced it unconstitutional; and that opinion being generally entertained, it ought to be solemnly pronounced by the Legislature, that history and the records of the country may not hand it down to posterity as a precedent for acts of similar usurpation. If a revision of the proceedings in that case was important in a public point of view, it was certainly so as it related to the individuals who became the subjects of prosecution under that act. To each of them, and to every citizen of the United States, the Constitution of the United States had guarantied certain rights, which had been violated by that law. This guaranty entitled them to indemnity in cases wherein those rights were violated; of this indemnity, the decision of courts ought not to deprive them. If they did, he said, there is no redeeming spirit in the Constitution. Legal sanctions cannot vitiate constitutional provisions. The Judiciary is a valuable part of the Government, and ought to be highly respected; but is not infallible. The Constitution is our guide—our supreme law. Blind homage can never be rendered by freemen to any power. In all cases of alleged violations of the Constitution, it was for Congress to make a just discrimination. In doubtful cases, he said, he would not interfere; but when the Constitution forbade a law, he would not hesitate to interpose for the relief of those who suffered by its inflictions.—*Benton's Abridgment, vol.* 6, *page* 184.

Nathaniel Macon, of North Carolina, on the same day, said:

According to some gentlemen, we were to regard the Judiciary more than the law, and both more than the Constitution. It was a misfortune the judges were not equal in infallibility to the God who made them. The truth was, if the judge was a party man out of power, he would be a party man in. The office would not change human nature. He had no doubt that the sedition law, and the proceedings under it, had more effect in revolutionizing the Government than all its other acts. He well remembered the language of the times—pay your taxes, but don't speak against Government. The gentleman from Massachusetts admits the inexpediency of the law, but not its unconstitutionality. This was of itself a great concession. Would he, or the gentleman from South Carolina, put his finger on the clause of the Constitution which authorized that law? He would not impute evil motives—he had nothing to do with them, but with acts. He would have preferred a silent vote; but, being referred to in the petition, he could not be silent. Money is paid back daily from the Treasury to individuals, without its being called revising the decision of the judges. He did not agree with the gentleman from Massachusetts (Mr. Otis) about the powers of the Government. That gentleman thought it might do any act necessary to its preservation. He (Mr. M.) believed it could not go beyond the Constitution. We have in the country two Governments. The Constitution defines the powers of the General Government, and leaves the State Governments untouched. He thought the position clear, that if there was no constitutional power to pass the law, the money was taken wrongfully, and ought to be restored. Mr. Macon was sorry the names of judges had been introduced. We ought to pass lightly over the ashes of the dead. Let them sleep quietly with their fathers. He would not disturb them.—*Ib., page* 187.

Extract from a report made to the United States Senate, December 5, 1820, on the petition of Matthew Lyon, by the Hon. James Barbour, of Virginia, in behalf of a committee of that body to whom the petition was referred:

The claim of the petitioner to redress rests on the facts, that he was convicted under the law commonly called the sedition act, and suffered in his body a long and loathsome confinement in jail, and in his estate, by the payment of a large fine. * * * A majority of the committee, after the severest investigation, have decided that the petitioner is entitled to relief. * *

The first question that naturally presents itself in the investigation is, was the law constitutional! The committee have no hesitation in pronouncing, in their opinions, it was not. * * *

The committee are aware that, in opposition to this view of the subject, the decision of some of the judges of the Supreme Court, sustaining the constitutionality of the law, has been frequently referred to, as sovereign and conclusive of the question.

The committee entertain a high respect for the purity and intelligence of the Judiciary. But it is a rational respect, limited by a knowledge of the frailty of human nature, and the theory of the Constitution, which declares, not only that judges may err in opinion, but also may commit crimes, and hence has provided a tribunal for the trial of offenders.

In times of violent party excitement, agitating the whole nation, to expect that judges will be entirely exempt from its influence, argues a profound ignorance of mankind. Although clothed with the ermine, they are still men, and carry into the judgment seat the passions and motives common to their kind. Their decisions on party questions reflect their individual opinions, which frequently betray them unconsciously into error. To balance the judgment of a whole people by that of two or three men, no matter what may be their official elevation, is to exalt the creature of the Constitution above its creator, and to assail the foundation of our political frabric; which is, that the decision of the people is infallible, from which there is no appeal but to Heaven.—*See Benton's Abridgment, vol.* 6, *pages* 660, 661.

Mahlon Dickerson, of New Jersey, said:

But I must beg leave to differ from the honorable gentleman (Mr. Walker, of Georgia) when he informs us that our independent Judiciary is the bulwark of the liberties of the people. By which he must mean, defenders of the people against the oppressions of the Government. From what I witnessed in the years 1798, 1799, and 1800, I never shall, I never can, consider our Judiciary as the bulwark of the liberties of the people. The people must look out for other bulwarks for their liberties. I have the most profound respect for the learning, talents, and integrity, of the honorable judges who fill the Federal bench. But if those who carried into effect the sedition act are to be called the people's defenders, it must be for nearly the same reason that the Fates were called *Parcæ—quia non parcebant.* It would be a subject of curious investigation, how far the Judiciary, from the earliest times to the present, have been the defenders of the people's liberties against the oppressions of Government; how much their zeal has been increased or diminished by the certainty or uncertainty in the tenure of office; how far by an increase or diminution of salary; how much it has been affected by a fear of loss of office or salary on one side, or the hope of further promotion or increase of salary on the other. But such speculations at present are unnecessary.—*See ib., page* 701.

GEORGIA.

In the case of Paddelford, Fay, & Company, *vs.* the Mayor and Aldermen of the city of Savannah, Judge Benning, in delivering the opinion of the court, recited two or three cases in which the State of Georgia had acted in disregard of the decisions of the Supreme Court of the United States. In the case of Chisholm, executor, against Georgia, the Supreme Court of the United States—

Ordered, that unless the said State shall either in due form appear, or show cause to the contrary, in this court, by the first day of next term, judgment by default shall be entered against the said State.

The reporter adds, in a note, that, "in February term, 1794, judgment *was* rendered for the plaintiff, and a writ of inquiry awarded. The writ, however, was not sued out and executed; so that this cause, and all of the other suits against States, were swept at once from the records of the court, by the amendment of the Federal Constitution."

Georgia treated the court with contempt in respect to this case. Her position was, that the court had no jurisdiction of *her* as a *party*.—*Georgia Reports, vol.* 14, *page* 479.

The Judge proceeds to say, that "in this position Georgia triumphed," and that the judgment against her "fell dead."

The Judge next cites the case of Worcester and Butler, who had settled on the Cherokee lands in Georgia, contrary to the laws of the State, and for which offence they were sent to the penitentiary. On a writ of error, the Supreme Court of the United States annulled the judgment in the State court, and issued a mandate to the Superior Court of Georgia, to carry its judgment of reversal into execution. Judge Benning proceeds:

Now, what did Georgia do on receipt of this special mandate? Through every department of her Government, she treated the mandate and the writ of error with contempt the most profound. She did not even protest against jurisdiction, as she had done in the case of Chisholm's executors; but she kept Worcester and Butler in the penitentiary, and she executed, in the Creek nation, the laws, for violating which they had been put in the penitentiary. * * *

Judge Benning, in delivering his opinion, says, further:

It was not only in this case that Georgia occupied this position; she did it in two other cases, and those, cases of life and death: the case of Tassels, and that of Graves. One of these happened before those of Worcester and Butler, namely, in 1830; the other afterwards, in 1834. The Supreme Court had issued writs of error in each of these cases, on the application of the defendants to the State of Georgia; but, as the cases are not reported, it is to be presumed that these writs never got back to the Supreme Court; or that, if they ever did, it was too late. It is certain that Georgia hung the applicants for the writ.

In the Tassels case, the Legislature passed these, among other resolutions:

Resolved, That the State of Georgia will never so far compromit her sovereignty, as an independent State, as to become a party to the case sought to be made before the Supreme Court of the United States, by the writ in question.

Resolved, That his Excellency the Governor be, and he and every other officer of this State is hereby, requested and enjoined to disregard any and every mandate and process that has been or shall be served on him or them, purporting to proceed from the Chief Justice or any Associate Justice of the Supreme Court of the United States, for the purpose of arresting the execution of any of the criminal laws of this State.

Similar resolutions were passed, as to the case of Graves, by the Legislature of 1834.

PENNSYLVANIA.

The Supreme Court of Pennsylvania, in the case of the Commonwealth *vs.* Cobbett, gave a unanimous opinion in 1788, from which the following is an extract:

If a State should differ with the United States about the construction of them, there is no common umpire but the people, who should adjust the affair by making amendments in the constitutional way, or suffer from the defect. In such a case, the Constitution of the United States is federal; it is a league or treaty made by the individual States as one party, and all the States as another party. When two nations differ about the meaning of any clause, sentence, or word, in a treaty, neither has an exclusive right to decide it; they endeavor to adjust the matter by negotiation; but if it cannot be thus accomplished, each has a right to retain its own interpretation, until a reference be had to the mediation of other nations, and arbitration, or the fate of war. There is no provision in the Constitution that in such a case the judges of the Supreme Court of the United States shall control and be conclusive; neither can the Congress by a law confer that power.—*Respublica* vs. *Cobbett*, 3 *Dallas's Reports, page* 475.

VIRGINIA.

The Court of Appeals of Virginia, in 1814, in the case of Hunter *vs.* Martin, devisee of Fairfax, entered the following unanimous opinion, after full argument:

The court is unanimously of opinion that the appellate power of the Supreme Court of the United States does not extend to this court, under a sound construction of the Constitution of the United States; that so much of the twenty-fifth section of the act of Congress to establish the judicial courts of the United States as extends the appellate jurisdiction of the Supreme Court to this court is not in pursuance of the Constitution of the United States; that the writ of error in this case was improvidently allowed under the authority of that act; that the proceedings thereon in the Supreme Court were *coram non judice* in relation to this court; and that obedience to its mandate be declined by this court.

RICHARD M. JOHNSON, OF KENTUCKY.

Mr. Johnson, who was elected Vice President of the United States by the Democratic party, represented Kentucky in the United States Senate in 1822. I find in Benton's Abridgment of the Debates of Congress, vol. 7, page 145, an elaborate speech of Mr. Johnson upon a resolution offered by him, proposing an amendment of the Constitution. His proposition was to amend the Constitution by referring all cases in which a State may be a party to the final adjudication of the Senate. In the course of his remarks, he says:

At this time there is, unfortunately, a want of confidence in the Federal Judiciary, in cases that involve political power; and this distrust may be carried to other cases, such as the lawyers call *meum et tuum.* It is the opinion of many eminent statesmen that there is a manifest disposition, on the part of the Federal Judiciary, to enlarge, to the utmost stretch of constitutional construction, the powers of the General Government, at least in that branch, and by consequence to abridge the jurisdiction of the State tribunals. I do not assert this to be the fact; but, if it is not, we should adopt some method, if practicable, to remove these ill-founded suspicions. * * *

Judges, like other men, have their political views. One may be friendly to consolidation; another may err on the opposite extreme; and a third may prefer that happy mediocrity, which is always safe, and generally salutary. When these are associated upon the bench, and each under the influence of his own partiality, there will inevitably be as different conclusions among them, where State sovereignty is involved, or the extent of Federal jurisdiction is called in question, as if they were members of a legislative body. Why, then, should they be considered any more infallible, or their decisions any less subject to investigation and reversion? Besides the differences arising from political prepossessions, the various structures of the human mind will produce a variety of opinion. One may take an expansive view of a subject, and base his decision upon truth and justice; another may be what is sometimes called a *technical judge;* and, though of equal integrity, may conceive it his duty to stick to the bark of the case, and confine himself, in all decisions, to the forms of judicial proceedings. This difference in the organization of the mind must necessarily result in a difference of conclusion. Courts also, like cities and villages, or like legislative bodies, will sometimes have their leaders; and it may happen, that a single individual will be the prime cause of a decision to overturn the deliberate act of a whole State, or of the United States; yet, we are admonished to receive their opinions as the ancients did the responses of the Delphic oracle, or the Jews, with more propriety, the communications from Heaven, delivered by *Urim* and *Thummim*, to the High Priest of God's chosen people, from the *sanctum sanctorum.* Other causes of difference might be multiplied to a tedious extent; but enough has been said to show that judges, who, like other men, are subject to the frailties, the passions, the partialities, and antipathies, incident to human nature, should not be exempted from responsibility on account of their superior integrity, learning, and capacity; or that their decisions should be subject to revision by some competent tribunal, responsible to the people. It is believed that this is the opinion of that great and good man who penned the Declaration of Independence, and who now enjoys, in the shades of Monticello, the blessings of the principles which it contains. * * *

It was the judgment of a court that doomed the immortal Socrates to drink the hemlock. When the Roman tyrant could no longer use a hired soldiery to immolate the victims of his jealousy, he resorted to courts of law. When Henry VIII, of England, would exercise cruel despotism under the forms of a free Constitution, the army, the court, and the Parliament, were the potent engines that sustained him. When Mary, his daughter, compelled the Protestants to seal their testimony at the stake, the court gave sanction to the murderous deeds. Her sister and successor, Elizabeth, created the Court of High Commission, and formally invested it with inquisitorial power. She also supported the arbitrary edicts of the Star Chamber. The Puritans, because obnoxious to the free exercise of the prerogatives of the Crown, were imprisoned and dispersed by process of law, and the judges were the supporters of her despotic power. When she would destroy her unfortunate kinswoman, the Queen of Scots, the judges were instructed to condemn her, and by their sentence she came to the block. This horrid deed was covered by the cloak of judicial proceedings. When Charles I determined to change the religion of Scotland, he made use of the Court of High Commission to effect the object. By the same judicial power, the advocates for the doctrines of the Reformation have so often been divested of their religious privileges, and doomed to seal with their blood that religion which bore them triumphantly through the vale of death.

These facts are not exhibited to derogate from the character of the Judiciary, but to show that no truth is more universally established in history, that no proposition can be more plainly demonstrated than this, that judges may oppress the people—that power cannot be safely confided anywhere without the guaranty of responsibility. * * *

But has this change in the judicial term, from tenancy at will to that of life, essentially changed the character of decisions in Great Britain? History records the mournful fact, that since the reign of William and Mary, the courts of Great Britain have invariably yielded obedience to the monarch's will, in criminal prosecutions. The banishment and death of many of the most distinguished of the friends of liberty will confirm the declaration. The honored names of Muir, Gerald, Margarot, and Emmett, with many others that time cannot bury in oblivion, must remain the monument of this independence of the British

Judiciary, which we are so proud to imitate. In controversies betwixt individuals, the effects of the change may have been salutary; but he who has depended upon the Judiciary to protect him from royal malediction, has leaned upon a broken reed. * * *

I know of no clause in the Federal Constitution that gives the power to the Judiciary of declaring the laws and Constitution of a State repugnant to the Constitution of the United States, and therefore null and void. No express grant nor fair construction contains it; and I presume every gentleman in and out of Congress will agree with me, that the States never designed so to impair their sovereignty as to delegate this power to the Federal Judiciary. * * *

The short though splendid history of this Government furnishes nothing that can induce us to look with a very favorable eye to the Federal Judiciary as a safe depository of our liberties. When a law was enacted in violation of a vital principle of the Constitution, that which was designed to secure the freedom of speech and of the press, the victims of its operation looked in vain to the judges to arrest the progress of ursurpation. If this power could ever be exercised to any good purpose, it would be, on such occasions, to declare the law unconstitutional which aims a deadly blow at the vital principles of freedom; but, so far as the transactions of that day are detailed in our public records, it appears that the Judiciary was a willing instrument of Federal usurpation. That law was executed in all the rigor of the spirit which dictated it. The turbulence of faction found no moderation there; and the people found relief only in their own power. The exercise of their elective franchise removed the evil, and this is their only safe dependence.

GEN. JACKSON.

The following is an extract from his message vetoing the bill for rechartering the Bank of the United States. It may be found on page 438 of the Senate Journal for the first session of the Twenty-second Congress, and is in these words:

If the opinion of the Supreme Court covered the whole ground of this act, it ought not to control the co-ordinate authorities of this Government. The Congress, the Executive, and the Court, must each for itself be guided by its own opinion of the Constitution. Each public officer, who takes an oath to support the Constitution, swears that he will support it as he understands it, and not as it is understood by others. It is as much the duty of the House of Representatives, of the Senate, and of the President, to decide upon the constitutionality of any bill or resolution which may be presented to them for passage or approval, as it is of the supreme judges, when it may be brought before them for judicial decision. The opinion of the judges has no more authority over Congress than the opinion of Congress over the judges; and, on that point, the President is independent of both. The authority of the Supreme Court must not, therefore, be permitted to control the Congress or the Executive when acting in their legislative capacities, but to have only such influence as the force of their reasoning may deserve.

General Jackson was aware that he had taken a strong position in that case; and he closes, most solemnly, with an appeal to his Creator. He says:

I have now done my duty to my country. If sustained by my fellow-citizens, I shall be grateful and happy; if not, I shall find, in the motives which impel me, ample grounds for contentment and peace.

PRESIDENTIAL CAMPAIGN OF 1860.

REPUBLICAN EXECUTIVE CONGRESSIONAL COMMITTEE.

HON. PRESTON KING, N. Y., *Chairman.*
" J. W. GRIMES, IOWA.
" L. F. S. FOSTER, CONN.
On the part of the Senate.
" E. B. WASHBURNE, ILLINOIS.

HON. JOHN COVODE, PENN., *Treasurer.*
" E. G. SPAULDING, N. Y.
" J. B. ALLEY, MASS.
" DAVID KILGORE, INDIANA.
" J. L. N. STRATTON, N. J.
On the part of the House of Reps.

The Committee are prepared to furnish the following Speeches and Documents:

EIGHT PAGES.

Hon. W. H. Seward: State of the Country.
" W. H. Seward: "Irrepressible Conflict" Speech.
" G. A. Grow, Penn.: Free Homes for Free Men.
" James Harlan, Iowa: Shall the Territories be Africanized?
" John Hickman, Penn.: Who have Violated Compromises.
" B. F. Wade, Ohio: Invasion of Harper's Ferry.
" G. W. Scranton and J. H. Campbell, Penn.: The Speakership.
" F. P. Blair, Mo., Address at Cincinnati: Colonization and Commerce.
" Orris S. Ferry, Conn.
" Abraham Lincoln, Ill.: The Demands of the South—The Republican Party Vindicated.
" William Windom, Minn.: The Homestead Bill—Its Friends and its Foes.
" Owen Lovejoy, of Illinois: The Barbarism of Slavery.
" Henry L. Dawes, Mass.: The New Dogma of the South—"Slavery a Blessing."
" R. H. Duell, N. Y.: The Position of Parties.
" M. S. Wilkinson, Minn.: The Homestead Bill.
" D. W. Gooch, Mass.: Polygamy in Utah.
Carl Schurz, Wis.: Douglas and Popular Sovereignty.
Lands for the Landless—A Tract.
The Poor Whites of the South—The Injury done them by Slavery—A Tract.

SIXTEEN PAGES.

Hon. Lyman Trumbull, Ill.: Seizure of the Arsenals at Harper's Ferry, Va. and Liberty, Mo., and in Vindication of the Republican Party.
" B. F. Wade, Ohio: Property in the Territories.
" C. H. Van Wyck, N. Y.: True Democracy—History Vindicated.
Hon. H. Wilson, Mass.: Territorial Slave Code.
" John P. Hale, N. H.
" J. J. Perry, Me.: "Posting the Books between the North and the South."
" J. R. Doolittle, Wis.: The Calhoun Revolution—Its Basis and its Progress.
" C. B. Sedgwick, N. Y.: The Republican Party the Result of Southern Aggression
" M. J. Parrott, Kansas: Admission of Kansas.
Federalism Unmasked: Or the Rights of the States, the Congress, the Executive, and the People, Vindicated against the Encroachments of the Judiciary, prompted by the Modern Apostate Democracy. Being a Compilation from the Writings and Speeches of the Leaders of the Old Jeffersonian Republican Party. By Daniel R. Goodloe.

TWENTY-FOUR PAGES.

Hon. Jacob Collamer, Vermont.

THIRTY-TWO PAGES.

Hon. Thomas Corwin, of Ohio.

GERMAN.

EIGHT PAGES.

Hon. G. A. Grow, Penn.: Free Homes for Free Men.
" James Harlan, Iowa: Shall the Territories be Africanized?
" John Hickman, Penn.: Who Have Violated Compromises.
" William Windom, Minn.: The Homestead Bill—Its Friends and its Foes.
" H. Winter Davis, Md.: Election of Speaker.
Carl Schurz, Wis.: Douglas and Popular Sovereignty.

SIXTEEN PAGES.

Hon. Lyman Trumbull, Ill.: Seizure of the Arsenals at Harper's Ferry, Va., and Liberty, Mo., and in Vindication of the Republican Party.
" W. H. Seward, N. Y.: The State of the Country.
Lands for the Landless—A Tract.

And all the leading Republican Speeches as delivered.

During the Presidential Campaign, Speeches and Documents will be supplied at the following reduced prices: per 100—8 pages 50 cents, 16 pages $1, and larger documents in proportion. Address either of the above Committee.

GEORGE HARRINGTON, *Secretary.*

www.ingramcontent.com/pod-product-compliance
Lightning Source LLC
LaVergne TN
LVHW020639110826
845149LV00004B/1290

* 9 7 8 1 4 1 8 1 9 0 4 3 9 *